Manage the Chaos, Bedlam, and Pandemonium

Planning, Prioritizing and Organizing Your Day in the 21st Century

Includes technology tips for infusing time management principles into Microsoft Outlook

By

Karla Brandau
CEO
Brandau Power Institute
www.itstimeforresults.com

The photographs in this book were either commissioned and paid for by Karla Brandau or purchased from various Royalty Free sites including the following:

- Microsoft Outlook Free Clipart
- DepositPhotos
- CanStock
- Fotolia
- Pixabay
- RawPixel
- Graphic Stock
- Istock
- Canva
- Wikipedia

Many thanks to cartoonists Theresa McCracken and Victoria Trum.

Table of Contents

Chapter One 1

   Is Chaos, Bedlam, and Pandemonium Your Constant Companion? 2

   The Story of My Life 3

   The Secret of Leverage 4

   Three Elements of Success 5

   External Problems, Internal Answers 6

Chapter Two 7

   Planning - The Miracle 8

   Self-Management - Not a Passive Art 9

   The Secret to Prioritizing 10

   Vital vs. Urgent 11

      Square #1: Urgent and Vital 11

      Square #2: Urgent but Not Vital 12

      Square #3: Not Urgent and Not Vital 12

      Square #4: Not Urgent but Vital 12

   Proprietary Model of Vital vs. Urgent 13

   Planning and Prioritizing Decreases Worry and Improves Productivity 14

   Tasks Move Up and Down in the Pyramid 15

   Sequencing: The Charles Schwab Story 16

   Summarizing the Charles Schwab Story 17

   Close Out Your Day 18

Chapter Three 19

   Take Time to Plan 20

   Concentrate and Focus 21

Planning: Right-Brain vs. Left-Brain 22

Right-Brain Mind Mapping 23

Left-Brain Goal Setting 24

Chapter Four 25

The Daily To-Do List 26

Digital To-Do Lists 28

Great Tools on the View Tab 30

Chapter Five 33

The Role of the Calendar in Time Management.................................. 34

Work "In the Zone" – Calendar Techniques 35

Mental and Emotional Factors 37

Meadow Lark or Owl? 38

Your Best Schedule.. 39

Chapter Six 41

Pre-Workflow Work: Change Your Time Scale to 15 Minutes 42

Workflow in the Outlook Calendar: Recurring Events......................... 44

Workflow in the Outlook Calendar: Productive Morning Hours............. 45

Workflow in the Outlook Calendar: Mid-Morning and Lunch Time 46

Workflow in the Calendar: Close Out Your Day 47

Plan Forward: Click and Drag Tasks to Another Day in Desktop Versions 48

Plan Forward: Click and Drag Tasks to Another Day in Outlook 365 49

Planning: Agendas and Notes in The Advanced Dialog Box.................. 50

Planning: Use the Insert Tab in the Advanced Dialog Box 51

Planning: Use the Insert Tab in the Advanced Dialog Box in Outlook 365 52

Plan Forward: Put Project Deadlines and Midpoint Checks on the Calendar 53

Planning Forward: Reverse Scheduling... 54

Chapter Seven *55*

Your Challenge: Leverage Your Time 56

Two More Tips 57
    1-Every minute counts! 57
    2-Stop Multitasking...57

Mind Map Template 59

Goal Statement Template 60

Strategic and Tactical Goal Statement Template 61

About the Author *63*

Karla's Certifications..65

Contact Information...65

Chapter One

Manage the Chaos, Bedlam and Pandemonium

"Guard well your spare moments. They are like uncut diamonds. Discard them and their value will never be known. Improve them and they will become the brightest gems in a useful life."

~

Ralph Waldo Emerson

Is Chaos, Bedlam, and Pandemonium Your Constant Companion?

This man has more tasks than he can handle. His sticky notes are flying everywhere. Look at his eyes: he is frozen in space. Transparency demands we admit we have been in the same situation.

How do you manage 21st century chaos, bedlam, and pandemonium? By increasing your understanding of time management principles and using these principles to organize your workdays. This book focuses on time management principles and the implementation of those principles in the tool of Microsoft Outlook.

A friend of mine always focuses on the tool, not time management principles. Before digital To-Do lists, he was continually disappointed in the work he completed in a day and blamed his tool for the lack of productivity. Thinking he would solve his problem; he purchased every hot new tool introduced to the market. Now with digital To-Do lists, he keeps switching software programs. It never enters his mind to learn time management principles.

Time management principles *precede* exceptional productivity. The principles I teach in this book are practical and tactical strategies I have practiced for years. They are not theory. They work!

If you have tried other systems and pursued other training methods and are disappointed with the results, read, internalize the principles in this book, and be pleased with the increased productivity you realize in your life.

The Story of My Life

"Oh, crap! Was that TODAY?"

These two woolly mammoths missed the boat...literally. In my opinion, other than making me laugh, this cartoon is about planning and meeting deadlines.

Sometimes we experience chaos, bedlam and pandemonium because we are not time conscious and lose track of approaching deadlines. We let the day(s) or the week(s) slip away, forgetting that the project deadline is Friday or Monday. We make a to-do list on January 2 and it's still good on July 2.

Don't let this be the story of your life. Read this book and implement the principles that daily keep you on track and help you meet obligations, keep promises and deliver results by the required deadlines.

You will never miss the boat like our friendly woolly mammoths.

The Secret of Leverage

Archimedes, one of the most famous scientists of ancient times, said, *"Give me a fulcrum and a lever long enough, and I can move the world."*

Even though I love an electric screwdriver because it makes me as strong as a man, I did not fully realize the power of leverage until I took my son to SciTrek, a science museum for kids, in Atlanta, Georgia.

One of the activities had three stations, each with a hundred-pound boxing bag but with differing lengths of the lever, as shown in the cartoon above. At station 1, we could not budge the 100-pound bag, no matter how hard we tried. Notice how short the lever is. At station 2, the 100-pound bag had a longer lever but try as hard as we might, we could only move it two or three inches off the floor. However, at station 3, the lever was very long and with one hand, we could move the 100-pound bag up and down at will. I will never forget this demonstration of the power of leverage.

The 100-pound bag you are trying to move includes work assignments, professional development, family, friend, hobbies, volunteer work – all the activities found in quality living. The fulcrum represents the tools you use to organize yourself, and the lever is the information I am giving you in this book. With the tool of Microsoft and the information you gain by reading this book, you will increase leverage and be able to move your 100-pound weight of work.

Three Elements of Success

Time Management Principles   Tool   Self-Discipline

Career Success

Career success begins with understanding time management principles. For brevity, in this book I abbreviate time management principles to TMP. Embed the TMP in your mind and awareness. Make them habits and you'll become an excellent time manager. To help you on your journey to time management superiority, the TMP are woven throughout this book.

The next element in career success is a tool to organize your days, months, and years. The tool I focus on in this book is Microsoft Outlook, but the principles work in many other tools such as Google Workplace. I give you tips on infusing time management principles into a tool and you may take the ideas and apply them in whatever system you are using.

After understanding time management principles and choosing a tool, you need a huge dose of self-discipline. I can teach you time management principles and how to efficiently use a tool, but I cannot give you self-discipline. That is your challenge and a test you daily face.

Great use of time means you have the self-discipline to "plan your work and work your plan," to quote American self-help author, Napoleon Hill, author of *Think and Grow Rich* which was published in 1937.

Planning your work is a strategic planning process that includes clarifying your long-term goals, or project assignments, and then breaking those goals and assignments into small chunks that you can put on a daily task list.

Working your plan is the execution process or what work you perform on an hourly basis.

External Problems, Internal Answers

How can this young woman look so calm when several people are demanding her attention?

I submit that it is because of the time management principle: external problems require internal answers. The four people, each competing for her attention, represent external problems. External problems can be too many interruptions, failing to prioritize and organize tasks in time slots, and procrastinating tasks until you end up in the crisis mode.

External problems cause us to *react* to the circumstances around us. Many think external problems are beyond their control.

Internal answers, however, give us the power to be **proactive** in handling external problems in an organized way. This young woman looks in control because she has internal answers that come from careful organization, meticulous planning, detailed prioritizing, giving associates a time slot when they can have her undivided attention, plus a variety of communication and conversation skills.

The strategies in this book give you the internal answers for eliminating chaos and remaining calm in the face of unforeseen bedlam and pandemonium, perhaps caused by others' lack of planning and proclivity to procrastination.

Chapter Two

Planning and Prioritizing: The Work of Worrying

"It does not do to leave a live dragon out of your calculations, if you live near one."

~

J.R.R. Tolkien

Planning - The Miracle

A friend of mine gave me this cartoon many years ago and I use it in my presentations because it describes faulty and incomplete planning.

Ben has done a great deal of work on his DECCO Project Plan. He has all the elements of success and he knows what the completed project should look like. But he has a problem with execution. He has penciled in: "Then a miracle occurs." The DECCO Project Plan represents our goals and objectives that are not well-planned, and we end up wishing there was a miracle to get us where we want to go.

It can also represent what we think we can get done by Noon when we are energetic and starting our day. When we only get 4 things done by Noon, we tend to get depressed because in our planning time, we did not connect the time it would take to execute the task to the time available on the calendar. We were not realistic about the "Complete" box which represents the itsy, bitsy time we have in our workday to produce.

We end up wishing there was a miracle and there is one. The miracle is planning and prioritizing.

Self-Management - Not a Passive Art

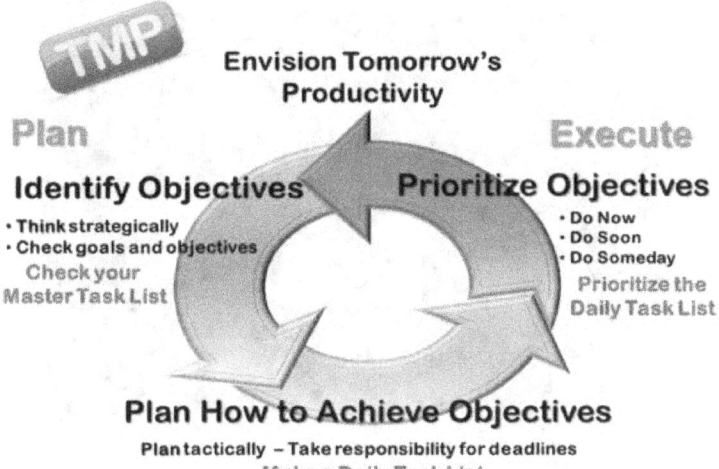

Self-management is not a passive art; it is an active art. It starts with identifying your objectives, thinking strategically about your goals, and putting tasks on a Master Task List. A Master Task List is a list of everything you must do to reach the goals you have set. It is the big picture such as the DECCO Project Plan the little guy made on the whiteboard on the previous page.

The next step in self-management is to plan how to achieve your identified objectives. I call this tactical planning and it involves breaking the goals into steps or tasks that can be placed on a daily task list with deadlines you intend to meet.

Finally, we get to execution. In this step you prioritize the items from your tactical planning. Notice the phrases that can help you with tactical planning: **Do Now! Do Soon! Do Someday. Do Now** means do it today. **Do Soon** means it can wait until tomorrow or the next day. **Do Someday** means it may never get done. Focusing on the **Do Now** means you are attacking the most important tasks for you to complete immediately – today.

The Secret to Prioritizing

The secret to prioritizing is to prioritize activities by the yield they give you. This explains why the **Do Someday** usually do not get done because the smart person focuses on the **Do Now** that pays the highest yield and the **Do Soon** that produces the next highest yield.

What is unfortunate is that most of us focus on the **Do Someday** because the tasks are fun, easy, enjoyable, entertaining, or exciting but they can be time wasters if they are unimportant tasks.

As you work through planning your daily activities, evaluate what tasks will give you the most return on the investment of your time or will contribute the most to achieving the success you crave. Prioritize them, then allocate your time accordingly.

Just like the little guy in our cartoon, most of us have many more activities we dream about completing than we have available time to work on. By prioritizing with the return on investment or the greatest yield for time invested at the top of your mind, you avoid getting bogged down in too many low-yield activities that deplete your time and mental energy.

Vital vs. Urgent

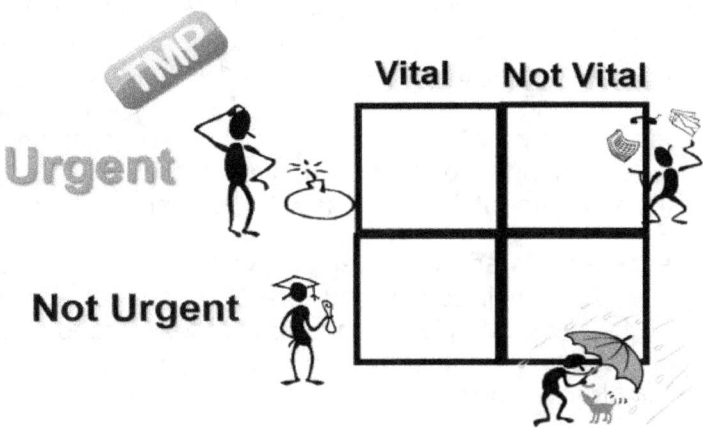

The **Vital versus Urgent Matrix** helps you sort out activities that yield the greatest benefit for the time you spend. It helps you calm the mental chaos.

Square #1: Urgent and Vital

When I facilitate this conversation in a live workshop, I ask the participants to put activities in each square. Some are baffled because they fill up the Vital and Urgent square quickly, thinking everything is Vital and Urgent. The other squares are blank. This is a fallacy.

If you believe everything is Vital and Urgent, you will work at breakneck speed, even on low priority items, often making mistakes and experiencing extreme chaos and bedlam inside because you just don't have enough hours in the day, hence the time bomb the string bean character is looking at.

Of course, everything cannot be Vital AND Urgent and as we talk about the squares, participants slowly begin to see how to prioritize and take control of their schedule.

The best way to explain the Urgent and Vital is remember your college days. You signed up for a class, attended the first session and the professor told you if you purchased his book and read it, you would get an A. Wanting an A, you purchased the book, took it back to your apartment and put it on your desk...where it remained until the night before the test. That textbook was vital the entire semester but only became urgent the night before the test.

Square #2: Urgent but Not Vital

The next square we want to discuss is Urgent but Not Vital. The Urgent but Not Vital represents many of the interruptions we get such as telephone calls, email, texts, and Instant Messages. It is interesting that digital interruptions are just as prolific as a manager, colleague or coworker stopping by your office, expecting you to stop what you are doing and have a conversation with them. These interruptions are urgent, but they may not be vital.

For instance, emails and texts demand your attention because you are curious about their content, but they may not be vital and thus when you turn your attention to the email or text, you lose focus on the urgent and vital task you were working on. It will take you several minutes to regain focus.

When a person stops by your office, cubicle or desk, they are urgent because they are standing right there, but her request, like a digital interruption may be less important than the vital assignment you are absorbed in.

Square #3: Not Urgent and Not Vital

The next quadrant to look at is the Not Urgent and Not Vital. Notice the umbrella and the little dog in this quadrant.

Sometimes we do things that are not vital and not urgent because they are quick, fun, and comfortable. We also put items in this square that cause us to relax, rejuvenate and replenish our energy.

This quadrant becomes a problem, however, if most of your time is spent in this square, such as swinging in your hammock and enjoying a great life. You are ignoring the urgent and the vital that determines your career success.

Square #4: Not Urgent but Vital

As we look at the Not Urgent but Vital square, notice the string bean character has a degree in his hand. Getting an advanced degree may be vital to your career but it is not as urgent as completing your assigned project by Friday.

Other items in this square include healthy eating, exercise, long range personal planning, self-improvement, family members, projects due in 3 months or 6 months, etc.

Proprietary Model of Vital vs. Urgent

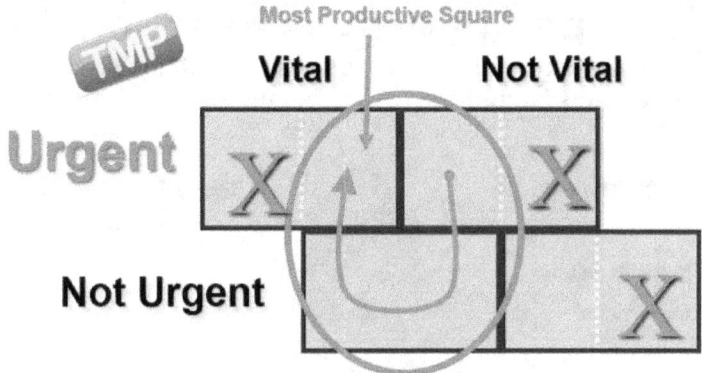

This is my proprietary model of the Vital versus Urgent matrix. First, I recommend you evaluate your urgencies and get rid of self-imposed urgencies such as procrastinating a task or not returning files to their correct place. One urgency you cannot eliminate is when your manager walks into your office and needs immediate help. Her request then becomes both urgent and vital.

In the Urgent but not Vital square, get rid of as many interruptions as you can by checking email at specified times of the day and letting your phone calls go to voice mail. In a similar fashion, in the Not Vital and Not Urgent, plan activities that relax you but refrain from letting it become a square for time wasters.

Let's pretend that a coworker, Patti, walks into your office and makes a request which is not as urgent as the task you are working on. You politely say, "I want to help you and I can help you at 3:00 this afternoon. Will that work for you?" Following the arrow in the diagram, you have taken control and moved Patti's request from the Urgent but Not Vital quadrant to the Not Urgent but Vital square. At 3:00 pm it moves into the Vital and Urgent square marked "Most Productive Square" where the task is BOTH Vital and Urgent.

The Not Urgent and Vital space is where you think strategically and tactically plan and prioritize in all areas of life. The Vital and Urgent square marked "Most Productive Square" is where you execute for excellent results.

Planning and Prioritizing Decreases Worry and Improves Productivity

There are three components to planning and prioritizing: value, urgency level, and sequencing. This pyramid illustrates these three components.

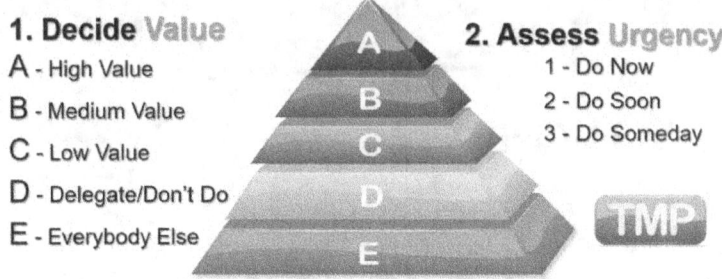

1. Decide Value

A - High Value

B - Medium Value

C - Low Value

D - Delegate/Don't Do

E - Everybody Else

2. Assess Urgency

1 - Do Now

2 - Do Soon

3 - Do Someday

3. Sequence **your top 5-6 items**

Deciding Value: in the 1950's in his book, *How to Get Control of Your Time and Your Life*, author Alan Lakein popularized the principle of deciding value with the **A, B, C** scheme.

A tasks have high value what **must** be done. They move your life and career forward. **B** tasks have medium value and **should** be done. **C** tasks have low-value and **could** be done. You **should** pay your electric bill or your electricity will be turned off. You **could** rearrange your sock drawer or sort your receipts.

I added Delegate because if you can delegate, this is the first thing you should evaluate when planning and prioritizing your own tasks. Delegating gives you time to focus on your high A tasks. I added Don't Do because often we work from the mindset that everything on our task list must be done. That may not be true. Evaluate your list and see if there are items you can eliminate.

If you do not plan and prioritize and identify the things that **must** be done**, should** be done, and **could** be done, everybody else will eat up your time and you'll be working for them and their priorities, not for you and your priorities. You'll be furthering their career and not your own.

Tasks Move Up and Down in the Pyramid

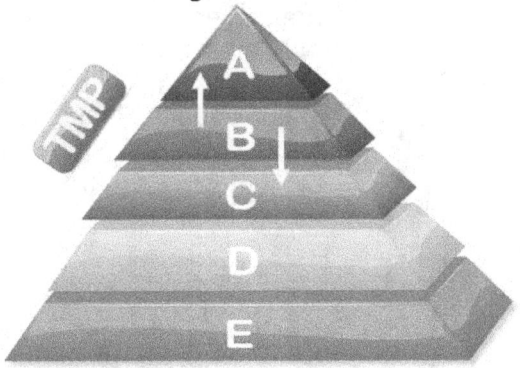

An interesting phenomenon is that tasks can move up and down in the pyramid, like tasks moving around in the Vital vs. Urgent quadrants.

If you have a task and are unsure of its value, mark it as a B. Why? Because a B task will either move up in the pyramid when someone asks for it or the deadline approaches. It will move down if no one asks for it or other tasks gain priority. If it keeps moving down and becomes a **Do Someday**, it will be gone forever.

At times, a task may move up so far it leaves the pyramid and becomes an urgency at best, a crisis at worst. A crisis is something that you can do nothing about such as God, weather, and taxes. Extreme procrastination on your part causes crises as well.

Working in the crisis mode can turn out to be counterproductive if the task is completed in a hasty manner that does not allow for checking spelling, grammar, statistics, and facts. Redoing and reworks waste time. As the saying goes, "If I don't have time to do it right the first time, when will I have time to do it over?"
In contrast, urgency has a positive effect on productivity. Urgency attached to a task moves you forward, triggers your creativity, and activates your problem-solving abilities. Attaching urgency to a task helps you meet deadlines.

Sequencing: The Charles Schwab Story

Charles Schwab

True confession, I was the girl in the 7th grade that had a to-do list stamped on her forehead, making time management a natural subject for me to teach.

When I started studying formal time management literature, I found a story of Charles Schwab in nearly every book I read.

Charles Schwab, was the president of Bethlehem Steel in Pennsylvania. Schwab wanted to get more done with his time, so he hired a prominent consultant named Ivey Ledbetter Lee. Schwab promised to pay him any fee within reason. Any fee within reason? Wouldn't that make a consultant's eyes get huge? Yes.

Ivy Lee studied Schwab and gave him this advice:

1. Before you leave work, make a list of everything you have to do the next day.

2. Identify your top 5 to 6 items you must complete tomorrow.

3. Pick your #1 task that you must complete and commit to doing it first thing in the morning.

4. When you start work the next morning, start with this #1 task and stick with it until you are finished.

5. Reprioritize the list and go to item #2.

6. In this way, complete the list. When this works for you, give it to your men. When it works for your men, pay me what you think it is worth.

This is not brain surgery. It is a simple formula to get more done in less time but it does require planning, prioritizing and self-discipline, the career success component we identified at the beginning of this book.

Summarizing the Charles Schwab Story

Before you leave work, make a list of everything you must do the next day. I call this closing out your day or COD. As you close out your day, you are making a master task list for tomorrow. Why do you do it before leaving work, or if you are working at home before you stop work?

Reason #1 - Because you want to capture unfinished tasks while they are fresh on your mind. As you go through your day, there will be items you do not finish, even with the best of planning. These items need to be identified as you close out your day and moved to tomorrow or another day in the future.

Reason #2 - Because you want to close the door on work and open the door to your personal life. This is important because everyone needs to have work-life balance and tend to personal living needs. Leave work at work!

Reason #3 - When I have a dilemma and can't decide a course of action and I crawl into bed; it is in the back of my mind. In effect, it is cooking on the back burner. When I wake up, inevitably I have an "Ah-Ha" answer. I know exactly what to do. I believe this will work for you as well.

In summary, identify your top 5 to 6 items you must complete tomorrow. This starts the process of prioritizing.

Pick your #1 task that you need to complete and commit to doing it first thing in the morning. To pick your number one task is the most important element of this exercise. The second most important element is to stick with it until you are finished, even if you are interrupted. This gives you closure and a feeling of satisfaction.

Reprioritize the list and go to item #2. In this way you complete as many items as you can in your workday. Then close out your day and get ready for tomorrow.

Six months later, Ivey Lee received a check for $25,000.00. This was in 1930. Today that $25,000.00 would be over $400,000.00. Charles Schwab said it was the most important thing he had ever learned.

Make this $400,000 tip work for you. All it takes is self-discipline.

Close Out Your Day
(And Clean Up Your Space)

As I mentioned, closing out your day, planning and prioritizing for tomorrow is not brain surgery but it does take discipline. I promise you, after years and years of practicing this, I know it works.

It is unbelievable, but even on the days when I'm out late and I think I'm just too tired to do one more thing, or I'm very focused on family or on a project, and I fall into bed without following this process, I am lost the next day. I look at the clock. It is Noon, and I haven't accomplished much at all.

Following the Charles Schwab process of closing out your day and planning and prioritizing for tomorrow gives you a starting point on tomorrow's productivity. You don't spin your wheels wondering where to begin because your planning gave you a head start on the day. You tackle the #1 item, check it off, and work through the day in an efficient manner.

It is a wise routine that helps you leave or stop work without worrying about uncompleted items. Those items are either on tomorrow's task list or captured on a future date to be revisited at the appropriate time. This routine is an incredible stress reducer and is totally liberating. Give it a try and enjoy your personal time.

Cleaning up your space, physical and digital, is also important. Clutter can distract you and be detrimental to your early morning productivity, as well as your mental health.

Chapter Three

Map Out Your Tasks and Projects

"Have a bias towards action – let's see something happen now. You can break that big plan into small steps and take the first step right away."

~

Indira Gandhi

Take Time to Plan

When you feel overwhelmed and are drowning in tasks, take time to plan. Break the tasks down into small steps you can put on a daily task list.

To emphasize the need to plan, ponder what would happen if you commissioned a general contractor to build you a new house and that contractor poured the cement for the foundation and started the framing crew without architectural plans. How do you think the house would turn out?

In a new house, such details as the doors, windows, electrical outlets and the WIFI are in the architectural plan. Proper planning ensures against costly errors and delays whether building a new house or planning your day.

The proper planning of your day precedes effective execution. Detailed planning focuses your mind, your energy, and your efforts. It helps you meet deadlines and evaluate options, improving your decision making and giving you the confidence that you are moving forward in the right direction. Uncertainty about the future is reduced as are time-wasting activities.

At the end of one live session, a man looked at me and said, "Karla, your main message is planning." I answered, "I've never thought about that, but you are right."

Concentrate and Focus

Time management training involves teaching how to avoid physical interruptions but preventing mental interruptions is seldom discussed. To illustrate how difficult it is to keep your mind focused, pick an object in the room and note the time on your watch. Now focus on the object until your mind wanders. When your mind wanders, look at your watch to see how long you stayed focused. Did you make it 20 seconds? If you did, congratulations.

I find my mind wanders when I'm not sure how to solve a problem or I'm looking for greater creativity. It definitely wanders if I am bored with a task. When in a state of quandary, my mind easily moves to "I wonder if Byron has answered my email," "Gee, I forgot to call for a dentist appointment," "I wonder how Mom is doing today" etc. and etc. and etc.

The benefits of planning and focusing are many. When immersed in proper planning, your mind is focused and if you have laid out your tasks in a workflow fashion, you reduce mind wandering as you move through your day.

Concentration and focus are the key to completing tasks with efficiency, producing a better work product and increasing productivity. Decide today to concentrate and focus as you close out your day and devote the appropriate amount of time to planning tomorrow's work.

Planning: Right-Brain vs. Left-Brain

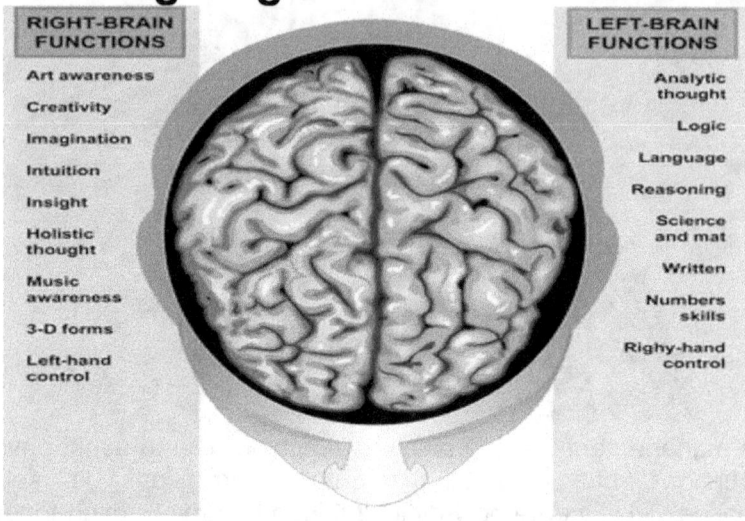

RIGHT-BRAIN FUNCTIONS

Art awareness

Creativity

Imagination

Intuition

Insight

Holistic thought

Music awareness

3-D forms

Left-hand control

LEFT-BRAIN FUNCTIONS

Analytic thought

Logic

Language

Reasoning

Science and mat

Written

Numbers skills

Righy-hand control

Now that you are convinced that more planning would help your timely execution of tasks, the question becomes how to plan and what tools you should use.

Some people are left-brained, meaning they are more analytical and methodical in their thinking; some are right-brained, or more creative and artistic, and others are an interesting mixture.

The left brain thinks in a falling dominoes fashion or in an outline while the right brain thinks outside the box, jumping from here to there, or bouncing back and forth like the eight ball on a pool table. Left-brainers think in words and approach planning in a rational, linear way. Right-brainers visualize the whole picture and look at problems from different angles.

I believe right brain people can learn from left brain people, and vice versa.

Let us look at a planning tool that works for both left brain and right brain individuals.

Right-Brain Mind Mapping

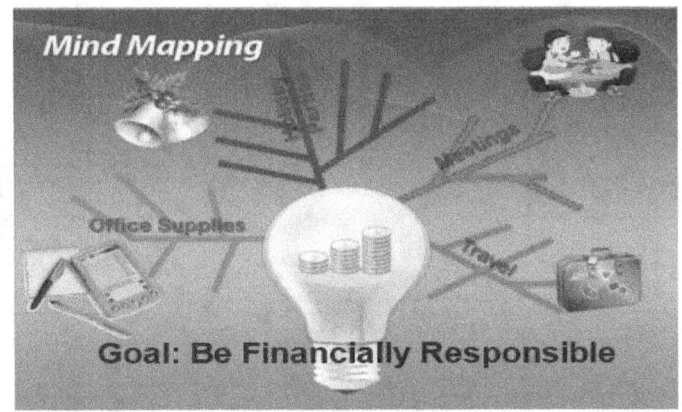

If you have never used mind mapping, I highly recommend it as a tool for getting rid of the chaos that happens in your brain when you are overwhelmed.

First, find a sheet of paper (I prefer a very light canary yellow color) and draw a light bulb in the middle. Across the light bulb write your project that needs planning. Here I have chosen "Be Financially Responsible." Next you decide the main subjects that need to be addressed which become the main lines coming out from the light bulb. For this example, I used Travel, Meetings, Holiday Parties and Office Supplies as key financial areas to be evaluated. As ideas come to your mind, put those ideas on the stems coming out from the main lines. This process keeps going until all your ideas have been captured.

The beauty of the Mind Map is that it captures the Macro view (the big picture) and the Micro view (the details). When all tasks or ideas have been captured, it is easy to turn to the left-brain process of putting the tasks in a numbered list or an outline. Even if left-brained people don't like it for organizing they see the value as a brainstorming tool.

How does this apply to planning? I often use a mind map when I'm overwhelmed with tasks for a single project or when I have several projects to finish in a week. It works magic.

Left-Brain Goal Setting

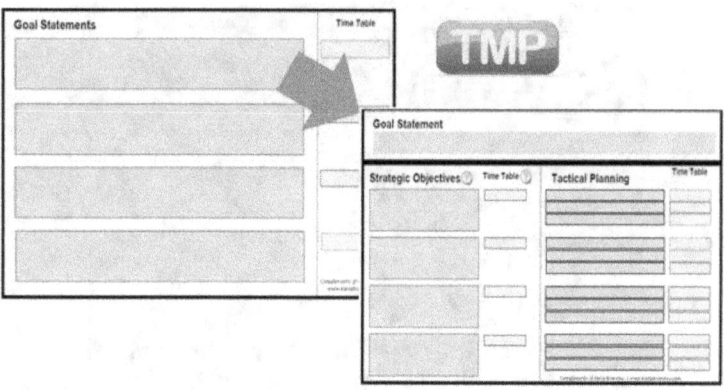

Whether you are left-brain or right brain, after the mind map exercise, you can use left-brain goal setting sheets. You begin with goal statements that have a date for completion identified. This sheet has room for 4 goal statements that are specific, measurable, attainable, and relevant to your workload, your career or your life.

After writing your goal statements, break each statement into Strategic and Tactical steps. Strategic objectives are what I want to achieve in the next week, month, or 6-months. Tactical planning is answering the question, "What am I going to do today?" Your daily task list is tactical planning in action.

The concept of strategic to tactical planning is to continue breaking the goal into smaller and smaller steps until you reach tasks that take 15-20 minutes. These small tasks go on a daily task list and turn goal setting into achievement.

Breaking projects and goals into smaller chunks take time but it saves time in execution. The process keeps your mind focused, allows you to measure progress, and helps you overcome procrastination. It gives you long-term vision and short-term motivation. This goal setting process improves performance, reduces stress, and helps you be more self-confident.

An interesting phenomenon is that you can't do a goal. You can only do the steps leading to goal attainment.

Chapter Four

Do More Than Survive Today: Thrive with To-Do Lists

"I made a huge To-Do list for today. I just can't figure out who's going to do it."

~

Anonymous

The Daily To-Do List

Whether you are left-brained or right-brained, make to-do lists a necessary part of your time management strategy. A daily to-do list is a must. It keeps the **Do Now** tasks at the front of your consciousness. Weekly and monthly to-do lists keep you focused on coming deadlines and eliminate memory loss or forgetting what is due when. In fact, a to-do list for the future gives you permission to forget.

Seeing a clear outline of what you must accomplish reduces your stress, your sense of being overwhelmed, and gives you a feeling of being grounded. Your to-do list is a tool to prepare for your future events.

Crossing off completed tasks is therapy for your soul. It means you have finished and achieved something despite human inertia and interruptions.

Another term for making a to-do list is planning. Studies show that just 15 minutes in planning can save one hour in execution. I recommend you spend 15-20 minutes at the end of every workday to plan. The term I use is Close Out Your Day which we will discuss more in-depth later.

When you Close Out Your Day, you automatically save time as you are not spinning your wheels wondering where to start the next morning. You have more brain capacity to focus because you are not trying to remember from the day before what you have to do next.

A well written to-do list helps you eliminate **Do Someday** and **Can Wait** in preference for **Do Now**. It helps you refocus your brain as priorities change.

Digital To-Do Lists

(For this technology section, open the version of Outlook you are using to fully understand the instructions.)

Pen and a yellow pad or a datebook organizer still work but a digital to-do list is superior. It eliminates rewriting when you are closing out your day and moving tasks forward. Technology can move the tasks to another time slot on another day as you close out your day.

There are many options, apps and websites for digital to-do lists. I recommend choosing a to-do list option that coordinates with a calendar as Microsoft Outlook does, either on the desktop or with Outlook 365 on the web. It is increasingly important that your software choice can be synchronized on all digital devices: phone, desktop, and tablet.

Closing out your day and moving tasks into the future helps prevent to-do lists that grow exponentially. It is important to remember the **Do Now**, **Do Soon** and **Do Someday** principles to keep to-do lists manageable.

A complete planning process includes daily task lists, weekly task lists and monthly targets. Future to-do lists can become tickler files, or entries waiting for you on your calendar that "tickle" your memory and remind you to complete them.

∨ My Tasks

To-Do List

Tasks - karla.brandau@outlook.com

DECCO Project

FML Project

Microsoft Outlook provides many ways to keep to-do lists. First, we will consider the tasks folders in 2013, 2016 or 2019 desktops. For clarification, the To-Do List is anything you have flagged anywhere in Microsoft Outlook. If you routinely flag items in your email, every flagged email will be on your To-Do list.

Microsoft Tasks is a folder where you create and control what goes on your to-do list. By right clicking you can add task folders as shown by the example folders, DECCO Project and FML Project.

Great Tools on the View Tab

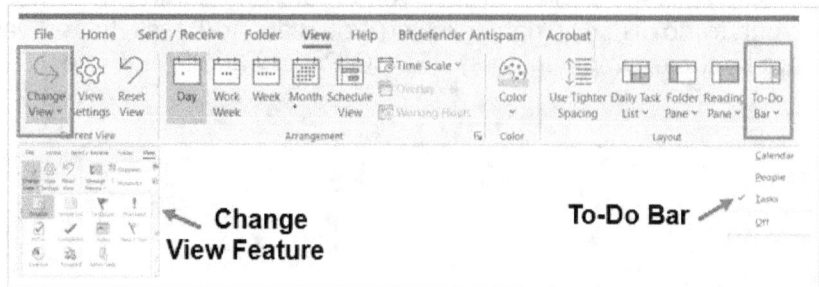

Change View Feature

To-Do Bar

The Change View Feature. By going to the View Tab, as shown in the picture at the left, and clicking on Change View, you can view your to-do list in a variety of ways. The Detailed View is critical if you are assigning tasks as it permits you to see who you delegated to, when the task is due, the status, and the percent complete, etc. Other helpful views are Prioritized, Active, Next 7 days, and Overdue.

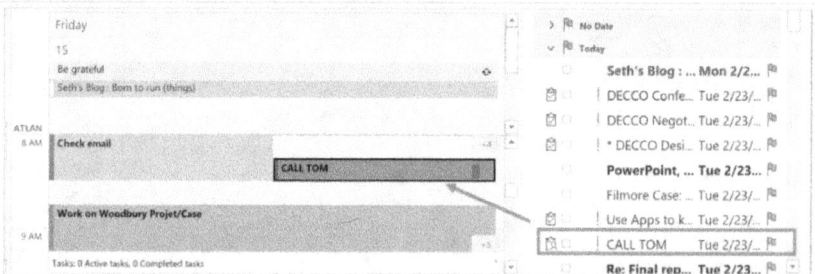

The To-Do Bar. The To-Do Bar is also found on the View Tab. It is an exact replica of the To-Do List but configured to show tasks by Due Date. The list becomes valuable as you sort email. When an email enters your Inbox, right click on the Status Flag and choose a list: Today, Tomorrow or a date in the future. If you choose the **No Due Date** option, the item becomes a **Do Soon** or **Do Someday** task, a **Master Task** list item.

The magic of the To-Do Bar is that it interfaces with the Calendar. In your **Close Out Your Day** planning time, you have the ability to choose an item from the To-Do Bar and click and drag it to a time slot in your calendar and into your daily workflow. This is very efficient.

The Microsoft To-Do App. This is a free app available on Android, Mac, iOS, and Windows. If you are using Microsoft 365 the To-Do App is a terrific tool. You download the app on your phone, open it and add tasks at will. They are on your phone and immediately show up in your Tasks in 365 Online. If you work mainly from your phone, your to-do list is always handy on your device.

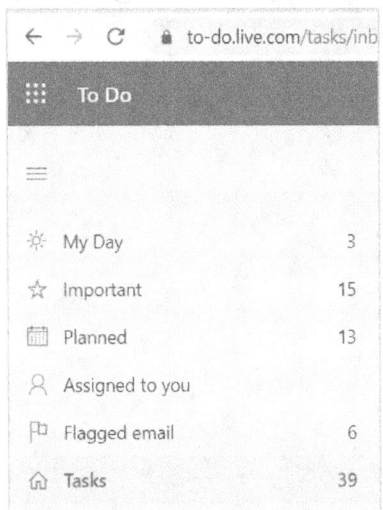

An attachment and a reminder can be added to every task. Plus, you can add steps to your task, a nifty feature when you are working to get complex tasks broken down into manageable steps you can complete in a 10-15 time slot on your calendar.

As shown in the graphic on the left, you can look at tasks for today as My Day, Important or starred tasks, tasks assigned to you, and tasks flagged from email. The House icon with the word, Tasks, next to it holds your entire list of tasks.

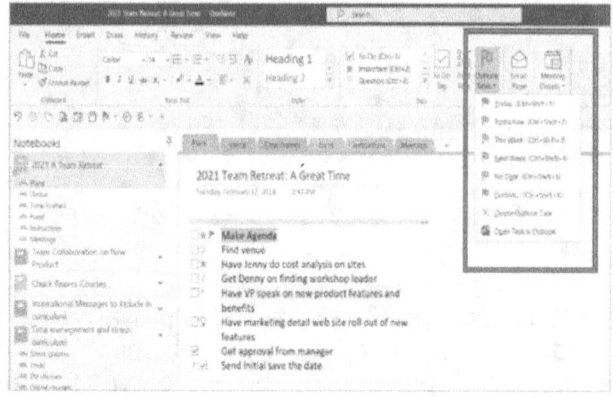

Microsoft OneNote. This software program is another way to manage to-do lists. It provides interesting icons for labeling items and setting reminders. If you click on Outlook Tasks and choose a day, the task will be transferred immediately to the To-Do Bar on your Desktop.

Chapter Five

Calendars – A Requirement for Time Management Excellence

"Don't be fooled by the calendar. There are only as many days in the year as you make use of."

~

Charles Richards

The Role of the Calendar in Time Management

An innovative way to look at the calendar is to use it as a workflow tool in addition to keeping your meetings and appointments. I have used it this way for years. I found that a To-Do list can be static. The old laugh line was you made a To-Do list on Monday and it was still good on Friday.

When I started looking at my To-Do list for major tasks and putting those vital, must be completed tasks on my calendar, I got more done. The important task was in a specific time slot waiting for me to start and complete. The point of the story? If it is on your calendar, it gets done!

The calendar now becomes a tool to manage your life, meetings, appointments, major tasks, and goals are all in one place.

In this chapter I give you innovative ways to use your calendar. Try the strategies and you will find that a calendar goes with time management like peanut butter and jelly make a sandwich. You just have to choose your jelly and the type of peanut butter you like.

Work "In the Zone" – Calendar Techniques

On July 5, 1975 when Arthur Ashe beat Jimmy Conners to win Wimbledon, he said he could have beaten anyone because he was "in the Zone."

If you are a performer whether in athletics or the arts, you know what "in the Zone" means. Your play rises to new levels. Everything is going your way. In basketball, you swish 3-pointers. If you are singing, your voice has an extra sparkle.

"In the Zone" means you are fully absorbed in a challenging task. Your mind functions at its peak. Time is distorted. A sense of satisfaction comes over you.

As a performer in business, you can have the same experience. Identify your task and put it on your calendar in a one-hour time slot. When the time arrives, restrict interruptions, ignore all the beeps, bleeps, buzzes, pings and dings coming from your computer or smart watch and focus on the vital task. Don't make your mind constantly fight itself, caught between wanting to focus, yet giving into all the outside sounds in addition to the inaudible yet pervasive mental distractions.

As you focus, you will slip into "the Zone" and enjoy the work. In fact, since you are not checking your watch every 5 minutes to see if the time is up, you may have to set a timer to remind you when an hour has passed. Because of your focus, you will be amazed that the time passes so quickly and may say to yourself, "What! Is the time up already?"

Because you have advanced what you need to complete, a simple contentment pervades the moment. This is what it is like to work "in the Zone."

Mental and Emotional Factors

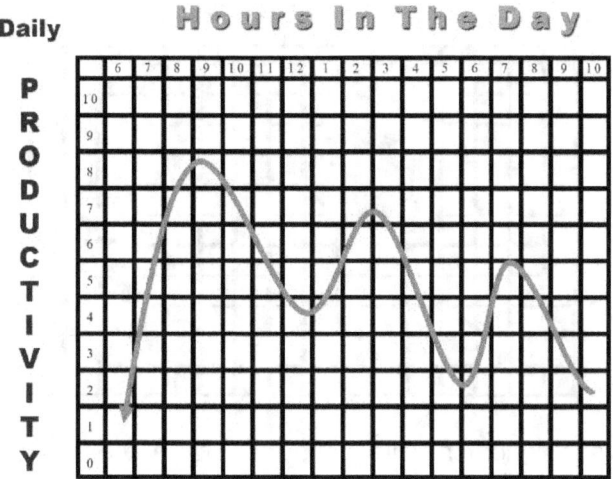

Daily

In this chart, the hours are horizontal and the productivity level is vertical. Your level of productivity is probably at zero when you wake up in the morning. In my live training programs, one person remarked, "Well, I am a minus ten when I wake up. I cannot get started in the morning." Another person said, "I'm definitely a zero until I've had my coffee."

This chart represents a normal human flow of mental and emotional energy. In fact, 8 may be high for some individuals on the verge of disengagement.

As you look horizontally, at the hours in the day, the goal is to identify your most productive hours in the day, when you are mentally and emotionally up.

Most humans are quite productive in the morning, then dip down at noon and then have a slight rise in productivity again in the afternoon with a big dip at the end of work hours. The dips are because we are not computers or robots. Humans need to eat, rehydrate, and rejuvenate their energy. A walk before or after your evening meal gives you another slight spike in productivity for the evening hours.

The goals, with proper planning and focus, is to raise your productivity level during the day to a 9 or 10 in the morning.

Meadow Lark or Owl?

I have a son who isn't his best at 7:00 in the morning but at midnight, he is brilliant. His is an owl. In contrast, I'm a meadowlark. I have always liked getting up early in the morning. Morning work fits my energy cycle perfectly.

Are you a meadowlark? If so, your mental and emotional energy is the strongest in the morning. Plan your most difficult conversations in the morning and tackle your most difficult task early in the day when you are emotionally and mentally energetic. Get started on the most challenging task as soon as you start work. Having tackled and completed the most difficult task on your task list in the morning frees your day up for conversations, interactions, and easier tasks.

If you are an owl, your most productive time may be after lunch. If so, tackle your most difficult tasks, projects, and conversations in the early afternoon.

The problem comes when there is a clash between owls and meadowlarks. You may have to flip a coin to decide when meetings are held. Meadowlarks may prefer the morning and owls the afternoon. If you are the manager, observe your people and schedule your meetings when it works for most of your team. If you schedule in the afternoon, make sure you have snacks available.

Your Best Schedule

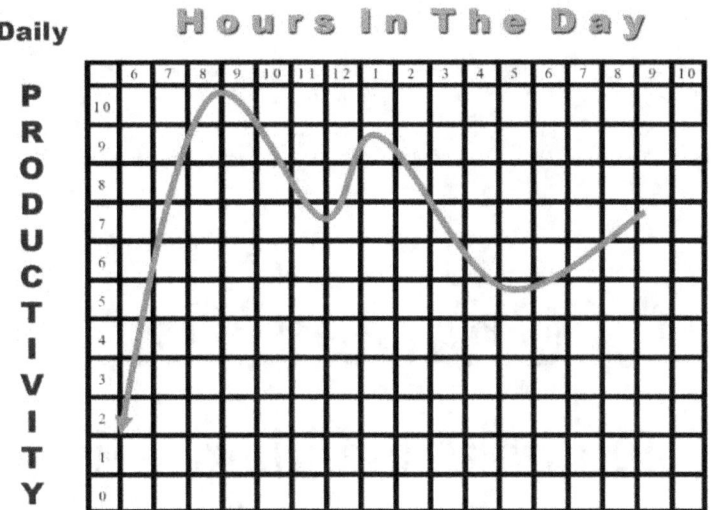

Whether you are a meadow lark or an owl, your day will have a natural ebb and flow - times when you are mentally and emotionally up and times when your emotional energy wanes. Learn to identify and work with your cycles.

When you are energetic, schedule your most intensive work. When your energy wanes, do the administrative or rote part of your work. Every job has routine work such as refiling folders or searching online folders, cleaning out drawers, returning simple emails, returning easy calls or checking on your Amazon package.

This graph makes you cognizant of your personal energy cycles and gives you a goal to use your energy in the most productive ways you can throughout the day.

Through proper planning, organizing and focus, and knowing what you will accomplish in each segment of the day, you will be managing your time and your energy levels for the highest productivity levels possible for you.

Chapter Six

Digital Calendars – the Alchemy of Time Management?

Alchemy: a seemingly magical process of transformation, creation, or combination

Pre-Workflow Work: Change Your Time Scale to 15 Minutes

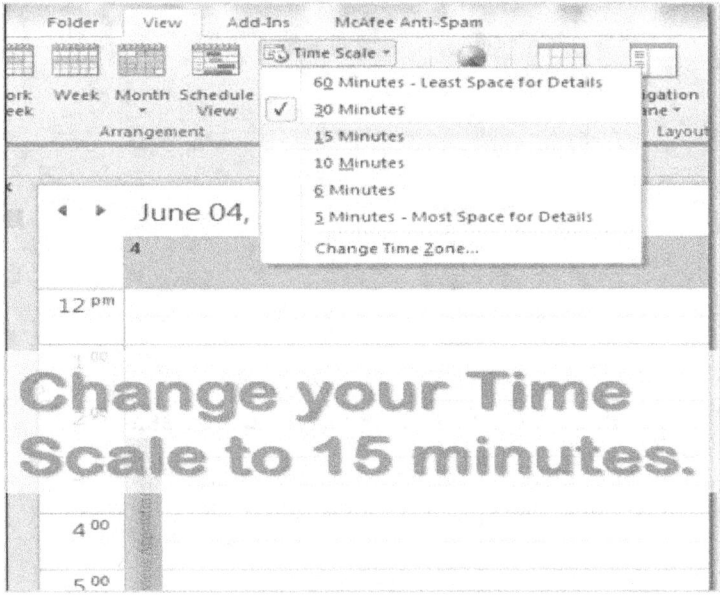

I recommend you change your time scale from 30-minute intervals to 15-minute intervals, allowing you to increase the number of tasks you can target for a one-hour time frame.

In the desktop version of Outlook, click on the View Tab in the Ribbon, go to the Time Scale and choose 15 minutes versus the default of 30 minutes.

This works in the desktop versions of Outlook 2013, 2016, and 2019.

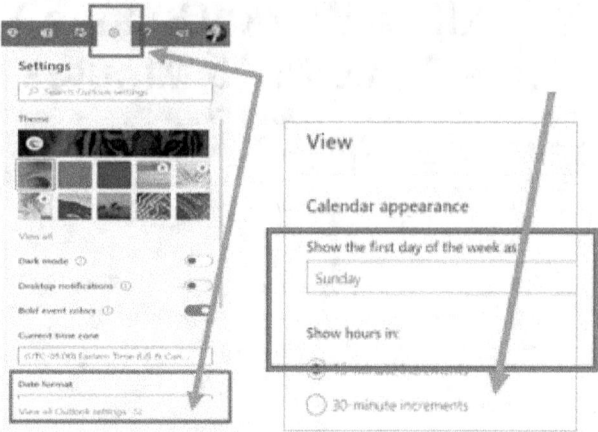

If you are using Outlook 365 on the web, click on the Setting's gear, scroll to the bottom and click on View all Outlook settings.

When the dialog box below appears, click on 15 minutes.

Workflow in the Outlook Calendar: Recurring Events

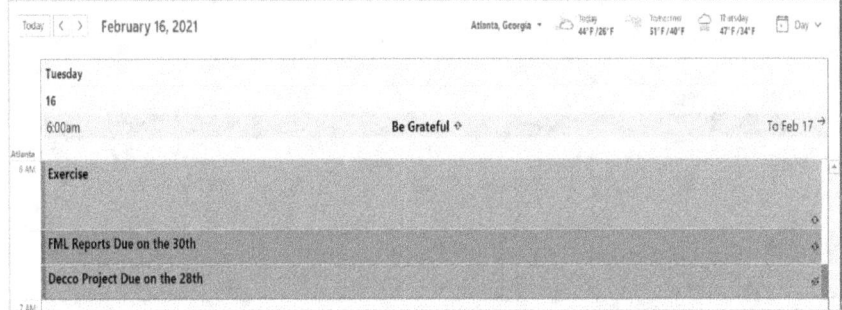

Making a task a recurring event, keeps you from rewriting or re-entering tasks.

In this example my first recurring event is a positive attitude and life balance issue: Be Grateful. This reminder keeps me focused on the good things I already possess, not my "wish list" of material goods.

Once, seated on a plane, another passenger walked by and the title of the book he was reading caught my eye: *Happy people are not grateful. It's grateful people that are Happy.* When I start to feel discouraged, this thought comes into my mind and as I list the multitude of family, friends, talents, achievements, and the material things that I can be grateful for, my happiness and productivity improve. As a recurring event, it reminds me every day to be grateful.

The next recurring event is exercise. I don't exercise to compete with the super-thin models because that has never worked for me. I exercise because it gives me more energy and helps me feel better about myself. I purposefully exercise in the morning to help me get the blood flowing and the mind invigorated. I believe exercise will do the same for you.

The next two recurring events are critical to my psychological and emotional health: they remind me of deadlines so I don't get caught like the woolly mammoths who missed the sailing of the Ark.

Other recurring events are helpful to keep your eyes focused on the light at the end of the tunnel.

Workflow in the Outlook Calendar: Productive Morning Hours

	Get Coffee, Chamomile Tea, or Hot Chocolate
8 AM	Check & Respond to Email and Texts
	Work on Section 10 of DECCO Project
9 AM	
	Agile Meeting on DECCO Project
	Check & Respond to Email and Texts
10 AM	
	See if Solar Panels have arrived. Call Geri - 770-892-5568
	Call Dan - 770-892-5534 - about content on website that is not uploaded Call Deepak - 770-356-9990

As in the Charles Schwab story, we have blocked a one-hour time slot at 8:15 a.m. for the most pressing task, the DECCO Project. Yet, considering the reality of our 21st century workplace, you get your favorite morning drink and check your email before tackling your hour long, focused concentrated work on the DECCO Project.

Notice the Agile meeting at 9:30 a.m. The power of Agile meetings is that they are short, 10 to 15 minutes. You get quick updates and status reports and then return to work.

After the Agile meeting, you check and respond to emails and texts again. Checking email should be done at specific times in the day. If you check email every time a new one enters your Inbox, email becomes an interruption. Next in your calendar are calls. Notice the calls are grouped together.

Grouping like items give you greater efficiency. The technique can be called "batching." When you batch items you group similar tasks and complete them at one fell swoop, avoiding the unpleasant chaos inside when you quickly hop from one project to another.

Workflow in the Outlook Calendar: Mid-Morning and Lunch Time

You may be surprised that I have added to the calendar Leave for Lunch and Return from Lunch.

Why? To gain the reputation as a professional, be on time to meetings. Notice the entry Leave for Lunch Meeting will go to your exchange server as Busy, making it less likely individuals will come to you needing your time while you are working to get out the door. It also reminds you to leave time for traffic, parking, seating, etc.

Return from Lunch reminds you how much time it will take to get back to the office. Upon your return, check your emails and get ready for the meetings you made with your direct reports (or colleagues).

In the similar way you grouped calls, grouping meetings is a time saver. Tell each person they have your undivided attention for their 15-minute meeting with you. They come prepared with their tasks and questions prioritized. Sanjay is first. He works through his agenda and as the conversation becomes superficial chit chat, Sara shows up at your door for her 15-minutes of uninterrupted time with you. Of course, Pat is at your door as Sara is finishing.

Automatic ending times for your meetings are created.

Workflow in the Calendar: Close Out Your Day

After the meetings with your direct reports, or coworkers, you schedule another hour of uninterrupted time to work on the financial portion of the DECCO Project.

As the clock moves to 4:30, you come to the most important time slot of the day: Close Out Your Day.

Even though we plan, days never go the exact way we intend. As you close out your day, you quickly check off completed items and you evaluate what was not finished because of interruptions, a change of priorities, of complexity. You move these items to tomorrow or another day in the future.

Following Ivey Lee's advice to Charles Schwab, you identify the top 5 or 6 A items you would like to get done tomorrow. This includes pinpointing the resources or B items that support the A items that need to be completed. B items can be considered subtasks of A items.

You prioritize and pick the number one task to start on in the morning. Put it in your 8:00 a.m. or 8:30 a.m. time slot on your calendar.

This process reminds you of how much work you have done and of the work that remains to be completed. As you close out your day, you realize you have worked hard. Now you deserve to close the door on work, let go of frustrations and anxieties and open the door to your personal life, knowing tomorrow's productivity will jumpstart itself.

Plan Forward: Click and Drag Tasks to Another Day in Desktop Versions

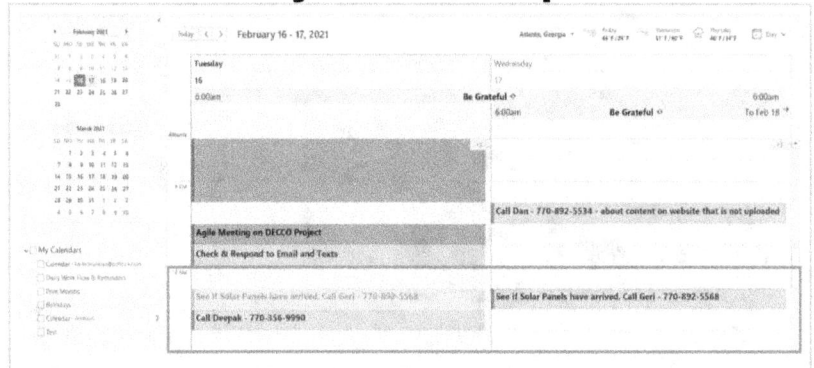

Planning forward, not procrastination, is a healthy way to look at moving the tasks you did not complete today to another day. Remember I said earlier that pencil and paper still work for a task list, but to move tasks to another day, you have to re-write every uncompleted task. In today's digital world, this is a waste of precious time.

A phenomenal feature in Outlook calendars, is the ability to merely click and drag tasks to another day. With this technique, you are not procrastinating, you are in control.

To do this in 2013, 2016 or 2019, open the Week view. Click on the task you want to move and drag it to a future weekday. It will be there waiting for you. You will bump into it at a more convenient time.

Another way to move tasks to the future is to have **today** open, then go to the date navigator (the calendars on the left-hand side of the screen), hit the Control key and click on any **date in the future, even in the next month.** That date opens and you have two calendar days side by side. Click on the task you want to move and drag it to the future day. Click and drag saves you nano seconds. You don't have to open the calendar item and change the start time.

Click and drag in Outlook 365 works a little differently.

Plan Forward: Click and Drag Tasks to Another Day in Outlook 365

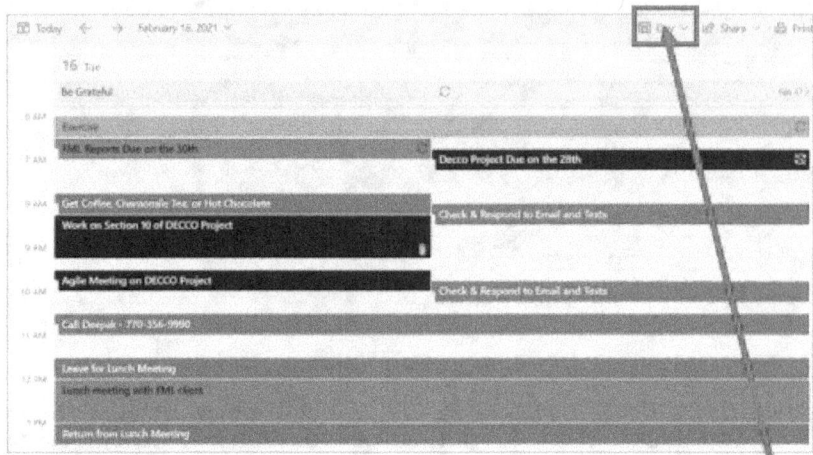

Even though this view is set to 15-minute increments, the lines are closer than in your desktop version. To click and drag events between weekdays, click on Day. From the dropdown menu, choose Work week.

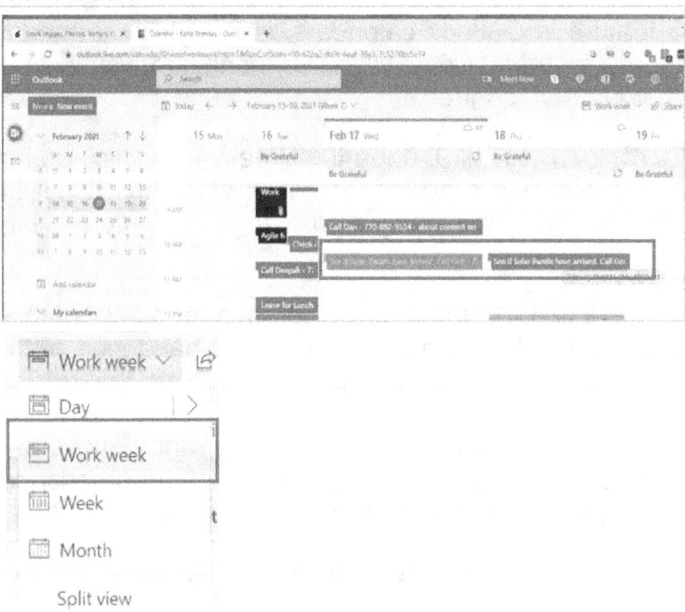

The week opens side by side and you can click and drag events from one day to another day in the work week.

Planning: Agendas and Notes in The Advanced Dialog Box

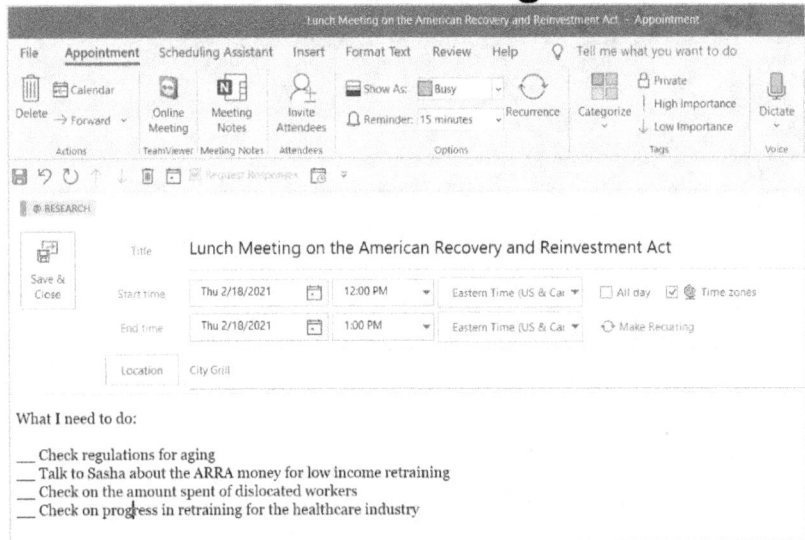

Many individuals I coach have never used the Advanced Dialog Box below the details of the meeting or event.

In this example you will be attending a lunch meeting on the American Recovery and Reinvestment Act. In the Advanced Dialog Box, you make a list of what you need to do to be prepared.

If you were the leader calling the meeting, you could start your agenda in this space. When you return from the meeting, enter your notes and document the decisions made. The information is permanently available, all you need to remember is the date the meeting happened.

This works wonders for planning future events, keeping notes, and reminders of what worked and what didn't work, in the same place. The event date never changes and the information can be retrieved by revisiting that date.

Planning: Use the Insert Tab in the Advanced Dialog Box

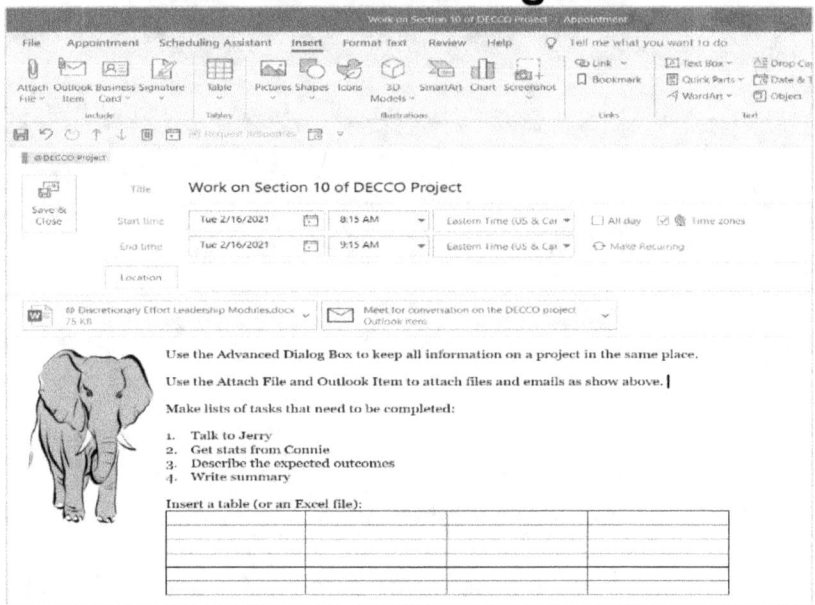

How do you eat an elephant? One bite at a time.

The application? When you are overwhelmed with a huge project, eat that elephant by using the expanded features of the Notes section of the Advanced Dialog Box by clicking on the Insert Tab in the Ribbon.

Notice the insert tab has the same features you find in Microsoft Word or PowerPoint. You can insert tables, charts, Word Documents, Outlook emails, etc. All the information you need for the project is in one place.

Planning: Use the Insert Tab in the Advanced Dialog Box in Outlook 365

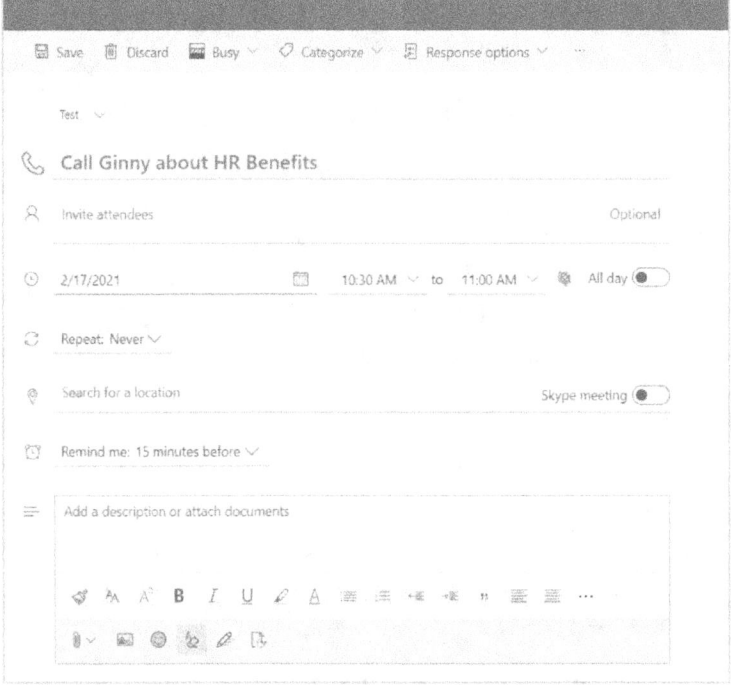

When you start a task in Outlook 365, the advanced dialog box looks different, but has many of the same features. Start typing in the box titled Add a description or attach documents. As in the description for desktop versions, you can organize a task, plan agendas and document information in this space.

After the task Is created, to add information in the Advanced Dialog Box, open it and click on Edit.

Plan Forward: Put Project Deadlines and Midpoint Checks on the Calendar

Today < > May - June 2021				Atlanta, Georgia · Today 44° F /22° F	Tomorro 51° F /4
Sunday	Monday	Tuesday	Wednesday	Thursday	Friday
May 2	3 9:00am 9:15am Start WHISTLER Project - Document the "why"	4 9:00am 9:15am Write the "how" for the WHISTLER Project	5	6	7
9	10	11	12 9:00am 9:15am Section One of the WHISTLER Project is...	13	14
16	17	18 9:00am 9:15am Sections Two and Three of the Whistle...	19	20 9:00am 9:15am WHISTLER Project Deadline for team m...	21
23	24	25 9:00am 9:15am WHISTLER Project DUE	26	27	28
30	31	Jun 1	2	3	4

Another element of ensuring your projects is completed on time is to put not just the deadline, but goals for completion at certain mid-points of the task.

In this example, we have designated the drop-dead due date of the WHISTLER Project on the 25th and then added what must be completed at check points on the way to completion. Be precise about what you are going to achieve in the time set aside at each check point.

This strategy gives your mind a goal. The human brain is a goal-seeking mechanism. For example, in your COD time, if you give your mind the goal of working on Section One of the WHISTLER Project at 9:00 a.m., strange, but at 9:00 a.m. you will probably be sitting in front of your computer, working on the WHISTLER Project. Even more interesting is that if you are NOT working on the WHISTLER Project at 9:00 a.m., you will feel anxious and irritated. Start work on the WHISTLER Project and these feelings dissipate.

An objective, a goal, a deadline, all move you into action. They give you the opportunity to focus and work "in the Zone."

Planning Forward: Reverse Scheduling

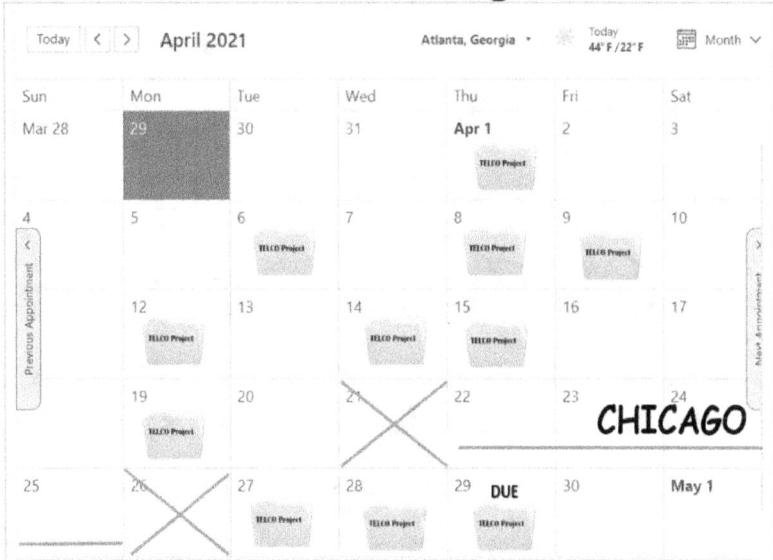

Planning Forward and Reverse Scheduling sound like an oxymoron. Reverse Scheduling could be called Reverse Planning. Let me describe it this way.

On April 1st you are assigned a huge project that is due on the 29th. You estimate it will take at least 50 hours of work. Using the reverse scheduling concept, you reserve 5 hours of work on the 27th and the 28th. Then in dismay, you see you are going to a conference in Chicago the 22nd through the 25th.

You mark out the 21st because of the details you routinely handle to get out of town. Similarly, there are usually fires to attend to when you get back and you mark out the 26th. You estimate the 40 hours left, considering meetings, appointments and other commitments and you mark the number of hours you need to spend on each day to complete the project on time.

Through this exercise, you are energized at the first of the month and focused on every workday, knowing the amount of work that must be completed to meet the deadline. You routinely work "in the Zone."

Chapter Seven

Will You Leverage Your Time?

"It takes as much energy to wish as it does to plan."

~

First Lady Eleanor Roosevelt

Your Challenge: Leverage Your Time

I have always innately known the value of good time management and throughout my life I have consistently looked for ways to save time on any task I approach.

When I study time management philosophies, a common thread weaves it way through the book: habits. Great time management involves improving habits. The principles in this book require you to evaluate time-wasting habits and replace them with habits that help you be organized and achieve the career success you desire.

I hope you marked the time management principles that can turn into solid habits and change your life, such as Closing Out Your Day and planning for tomorrow's productivity.

Some people resist the concept of planning the workflow of tomorrow's day because the plan always seems to get blown away with emergencies and interruptions. They ask, "So why plan?" Because when your plan is interrupted and you return to your tasks, you look at the next item on your workflow calendar or on your To-Do list, and you are quickly back on track.

I admit, most days will not flow perfectly as you planned, but some will. When that happens, you will be supremely satisfied.

If you plan, you can go far in life. If you do not plan, you risk a life filled with chaos, bedlam and pandemonium.

After reading this book, you have a knowledge of Time Management Principles and how to infuse those principles into the tool of Microsoft Outlook.

I now pass the time management baton to you.

With this knowledge, make every day count.

Go to www.KarlaBrandau.com for Time Management and Microsoft Outlook online classes.

Two More Tips

1-Every minute counts!

One statement that irritates me is "I can't do anything. I only have 10 minutes."

What a mistake. In 10 minutes, you can make a peanut butter and jelly sandwich and enjoy it with a nice tall glass of milk.

Research shows that people are interrupted every 9 to 10 minutes. When in the tactical planning stage, it pays to break tasks into 10-15- minute increments so the interruptions are not so disruptive. You will be richly rewarded as you complete many tasks in that 10 minutes you thought you could do nothing with.

2-Stop Multitasking.

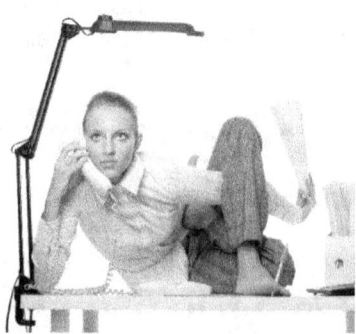

Stop multitasking because your brain monotasks!

You think you are watching TV and reading your texts or email but your brain is either reading texts and emails or watching TV.

Multitasking only works when you are jogging and listening to podcasts or sending a document to the printer while you return emails.

Multitasking reduces your ability to focus and studies show that focused work hours can yield up to 500% more results than non-focused, interrupted, and multi-tasking work time.

Mind Map Template

Use this as a template to make your own Mind Maps.

InfoMap

Compliments of Karla Brandau
www.KarlaBrandau.com

"Mind maps work the way the brain works -- which is not in nice, neat lines."

~

Peter Russell

Goal Statement Template

Use this as a model to make your own Goal Statement template.

Goal Statements	Time Table

"The harder you work for something, the greater you'll feel
when you achieve it."

~

Anonymous

Strategic and Tactical Goal Statement Template

Using this template, choose one goal statement and break it into Strategic Objectives with a time table. Breaking Strategic Objectives into Tactical Planning steps, each with a time table ensure you will reach your goal.

Goal Statement			
Strategic Objectives ⑦	Time Table ⑦	**Tactical Planning**	Time Table

"If you really want to do something, you'll find a way. If you don't, you'll find an excuse."

~

Jim Rohn

"Look at a day when you are supremely satisfied at the end. It's not a day when you lounge around doing nothing; it's a day you've had everything to do and you've done it."

~

Margaret Thatcher
First Female Prime Minister of the United Kingdom
1979-1990

About the Author
Karla Brandau, CEO of Brandau Power

As an internationally known keynote speaker, author, and consultant, Karla is a thought leader with a clarion voice in an often-ambiguous environment. She marks a clear path to leadership excellence and organizational successes as she challenges leaders to proactively remove administrative obstacles to productivity and implement true employee engagement practices.

Her mission is to inspire individuals with the knowledge and techniques to handle 21st-century leadership challenges while maintaining positive belief in the future's enormous potential. This mission led her to found her own company dedicated to building an organization's most important resource: its people.

Fortune 100 companies, national associations, government agencies, and educational institutions look to Karla as a keynote speaker and workshop leader to help them build productive cultures where conflict turns to collaboration and problems find innovative solutions.

As a Keynote Speaker, Karla spreads infectious enthusiasm for life while lacing her presentations with humor. She provides real help, not theory, for making goals and dreams a reality. She gives audience members the tools and techniques for professional development that will catapult them to achievers' upper echelon.

Her books are filled with no-nonsense techniques that give you strategies for instant implementation.

Books Karla has written:

- **How to Manage the Chaos, Bedlam and Pandemonium** is a targeted guide for planning and executing your day for infinite personal productivity.

- **How to Earn the Gift of Discretionary Effort** is a road map for leaders on charismatic leadership and employee engagement.

- **Wake Up the Winner Inside** helps you live your life with positive expectation which eliminates pity parties and bad attitudes.

- **101 Time Management Tips for Busy Professionals** tells you how to have more day at the end of your day.

Karla is reliable, versatile, and easy to work with — a hassle-free speaker — described as high-content, high-energy, and highly professional. To her credit, over 85% of the organizations who hire Karla invite her back for repeat engagements.

As a leading authority on building better business relationships and enhancing organizational productivity, Karla combines an engaging charisma, memorable stories, and delightful humor as she works her craft into a unique style that consistently gets rave reviews.

Karla's philosophy is that when you live with positive expectations and work as if there is no other option, success will come to you in a magical, mystical way. It has worked for her, and it will work for you as a leader, a manager, a team member, an employee, and as a human being!

On the personal side, Karla has been married for over 30 years to the same man. She has three children and ten grandchildren, making her a veteran of living life and surviving in all types of situations. She is a proven commodity when it comes to balancing life.

Karla's Certifications

- EQi-2.0
- Certified Facilitator
- CSP – Certified Speaking Professional
- RCC – Registered Corporate Coach
- CPBA – Certified Professional Behavioral Analyst
- CPMA – Certified Professional Motivators Analyst

Contact Information

Email: Karla@KarlaBrandau.com
Office Phone: 770-923-0883
Cell Phone: 770-329-1806

Web Sites:
www.ItsTimeForResults.com
www.KarlaBrandau.com.com
www.DiscretionaryEffortLeadership.com

LinkedIn: http://www.linkedin.com/in/karlabrandau

Contact Karla for customized coaching and training on these topics:

- Time Management and Team Productivity
- Time Management and Microsoft Outlook
- Surviving Email
- DISC and Driving Forces programs and certification
- Emotional Intelligence training and coaching
- Earn the Gift management certificate
- Build a culture of discretionary effort

Go to www.KarlaBrandau.com for Time Management and Microsoft Outlook online classes.